To All Children

Illustrations and Artwork by
Zeinab Shalaby, Hossam El Mouelhi, and Donia Farouk

Edited by Wafaa Shalaby and Noha Elmouelhi

Second edition 2023
ISBN 978-1-959536-01-7

Published by Honey Elm Books LLC
www.HoneyElmBooks.com

Alhamdulillah

الحمد لله

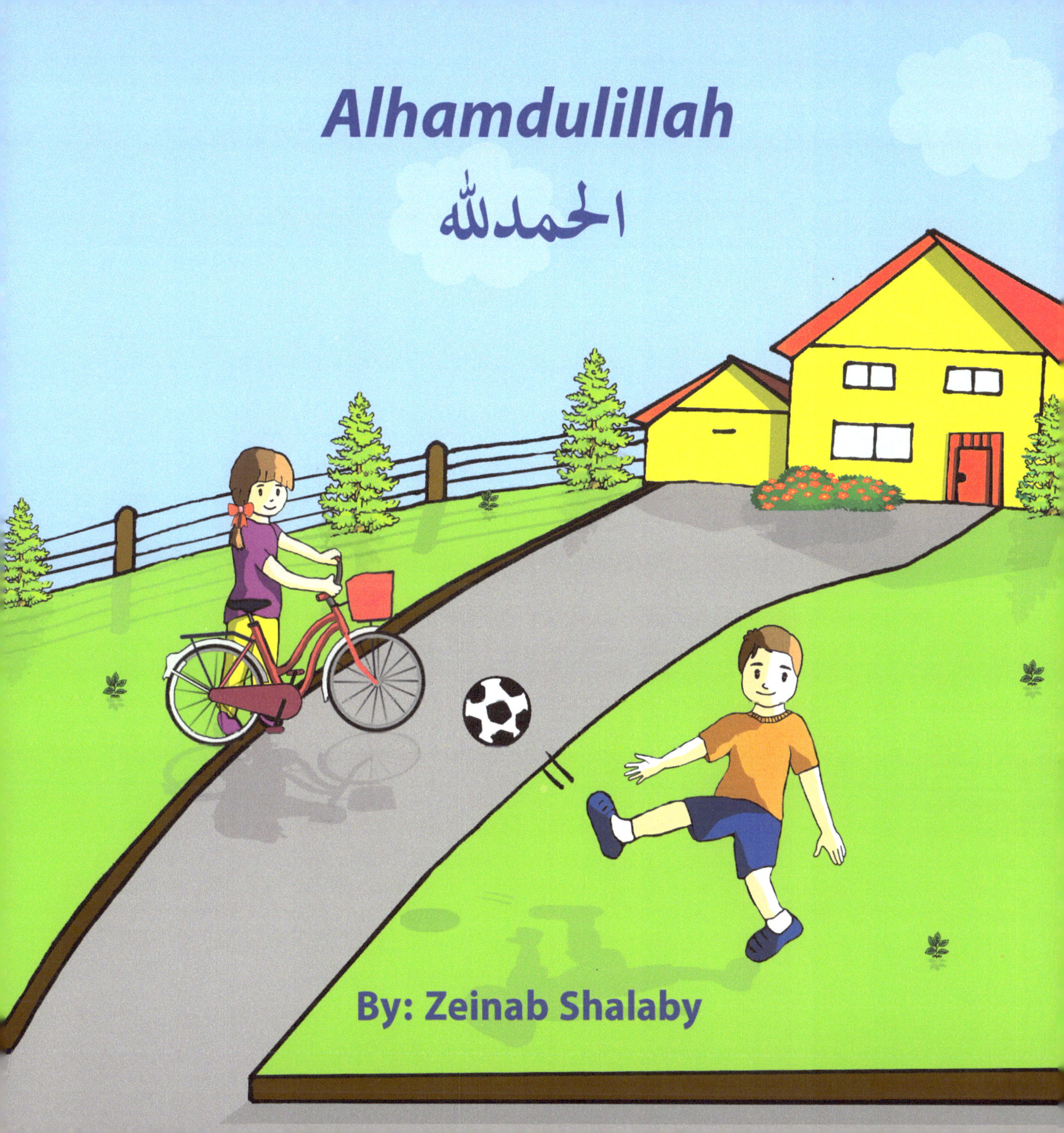

By: Zeinab Shalaby

Every day I wake up and say "Alhamdulillah (Thank God)".

I have so many wonderful things
to be thankful for.

I have a loving family.

We take care of each other.

We have delicious food.

We love to share it with our family

and friends.

I can run.

I can jump.

I can go down the blue slide.

I ride the bus to school.

I learn so many new things.

I love the snow.

My winter coat keeps me

nice and warm.

I am so thankful for all the blessings from Allah (SWT).

Alhamdulillah.

الحمد لله.

www.ingramcontent.com/pod-product-compliance
Lightning Source LLC
Chambersburg PA
CBHW041614120626
46551CB00002B/436